THE

LITTLE LOCAL

PORTLAND

COOKBOOK

THE

LITTLE LOCAL

PORTLAND

COOKBOOK

Recipes for Classic Dishes

DANIELLE CENTONI

THE COUNTRYMAN PRESS
A division of W. W. Norton & Company
Independent Publishers Since 1923

For information about permission to reproduce selections from this book,
write to Permissions, The Countryman Press,
500 Fifth Avenue, New York, NY 10110

For information about special discounts for bulk purchases, please contact
W. W. Norton Special Sales at specialsales@wwnorton.com or 800-233-4830

Manufacturing by Versa Press
Book design by Debbie Berne
Production manager: Devon Zahn

Library of Congress Cataloging-in-Publication Data

Names: Centoni, Danielle, author.
Title: The little local Portland cookbook : recipes for classic dishes / Danielle
    Centoni.
Description: New York, NY : Countryman Press, a division of W. W. Norton
    & Company Independent Publishers Since 1923, [2019] | Includes index.
Identifiers: LCCN 2019006341 | ISBN 9781682684214 (hardcover)
Subjects: LCSH: Cooking—Oregon—Portland. | Cooking, American—
    Pacific
Northwest style. | Cuisine—Oregon—Portland. | LCGFT: Cookbooks.
Classification: LCC TX715.2.P32 C46 2019 | DDC 641.59795/49—dc23
LC record available at https://lccn.loc.gov/2019006341

The Countryman Press
www.countrymanpress.com

A division of W. W. Norton & Company, Inc.
500 Fifth Avenue, New York, NY 10110
www.wwnorton.com

10 9 8 7 6 5 4 3 2 1

CONTENTS

Introduction... 8

Cocktails and Appetizers

Rosy Wine Spritzers... 12

Bandon Breeze.. 13

Northwest Shandy... 15

Fully Loaded Bloody Marys 16

Flaming Spanish Mocha.. 17

Brown Butter Chanterelle Crostini 18

Oysters with Cucumber Mignonette.......................... 20

Oregon Truffle Gougères.. 21

Salads and Sandwiches

Butter Lettuce Salad with Summer Fruits
and Hazelnut Vinaigrette...................................... 26

Kale Caesar Salad with Roasted Delicata
and Levain Croutons 28

Salade Niçoise Skewers with Fresh
Oregon Albacore.. 30

Easy Ham and Pâté Bánh Mì 32

Pub Burgers with Bacon and Beer Cheese 34

Main Dishes

Beef and Roasted Root Stew with Black Butte Porter 38

Dungeness Crab Cioppino 41

Northwest Salmon and Smoked Trout Chowder 43

Cabbage, Kielbasa, and Sauerkraut Soup 45

Baked Chicken with Kale and Cranberry Panade 47

Wild Mushroom and Pancetta Risotto 49

Cedar-Plank Salmon 51

Barley, Kale, and Freekeh Bowls with Lemony
Tali Sauce 53

Breakfast and Brunch

Buckwheat Porridge with Chai Pear Compote 58

Cornmeal Pancakes with Huckleberry Syrup 60

Salmon Hash with Double-Mustard Vinaigrette 63

Baked Apple Cider Doughnuts................................65

Desserts

Oregon Snowball Cookies 70

Almond-Matcha Madeleines with Cardamom 72

Skillet Marionberry-Blueberry Cobbler 74

Rich Mocha Puddings with Boozy

Whipped Cream 76

Acknowledgments...78

Index 79

INTRODUCTION

Neatly tucked at the confluence of two salmon-rich rivers, encircled by farms and forests, and less than 100 miles from the ocean, Portland is perfectly positioned as a culinary paradise. Here, we can hike into the woods and come back with mushrooms for dinner. A day trip to the coast yields a cooler full of crab and fish. And almost everything we crave thrives in our fertile Willamette Valley soils, filling our glasses with world-renowned wines and our near-daily farmers' markets with abundance.

Of course, it's what we do with all that bounty that's made Portland a must-visit town for food lovers. Our local breweries, neighborhood cafes, corner bakeries, and grab-and-go food trucks thrum with the kind of talent and creativity usually only found in big-city kitchens. And yet there's a particular flavor to it all, a fresh culinary style and independent spirit that goes big on experimentation, low on fuss.

Best of all, supplying these talents is an army of dreamers who are also doers, people who aren't afraid to jump into their passions with both feet to bring us things like exquisitely blended teas, artisan cheeses,

boundary-pushing spirits, and artfully crafted charcuterie. As the award-winning fruits of their labor find their way into menus, markets, and home kitchens all over town, it's easy to see why Portland has earned its reputation as a top food destination.

The recipes in this book celebrate the makers, growers, and ingredients that set Portland apart. Sip a riff on the flaming boozy coffee from the city's oldest restaurant. Bring the brew pub home with a burger spiked with beer. Re-create an iconic bowl from one of Portland's most successful food carts. Bake up cookies scented like a walk through the evergreens. Whatever you choose to make from these pages, you'll get a taste of what makes life in the Rose City such a delicious adventure.

COCKTAILS
AND
APPETIZERS

ROSY WINE SPRITZERS

Makes 1 serving

Raise a glass to the City of Roses with this pale pink summery sipper. In this drink, a slightly sweet, Riesling-based white wine provides the perfect fruity-floral backdrop to the bright-pink strawberry-rose petal syrup. I make the syrup in the summer, when Oregon's famously sweet and delicate Hood strawberries are at their peak. The syrup is also wonderful in milkshakes and smoothies. Look for dried rose petals at tea shops and find rosewater in gourmet shops or Middle Eastern markets.

FOR THE STRAWBERRY-ROSE SYRUP

1 pint strawberries, sliced (about 2 cups)

1 cup granulated sugar

½ cup dried rose petals

2 teaspoons rosewater

FOR THE SPRITZER

4 ounces ice-cold white wine, preferably one made with Riesling grapes

2 teaspoons strawberry-rose syrup

2 ounces ice-cold seltzer water

Garnish: rose petal, sliced strawberry, or lemon twist

Make the strawberry-rose syrup:

1 In a medium saucepan over medium heat, bring the strawberries and 2 cups water to a simmer. Cook, stirring occasionally, until the strawberries look pale and flabby and have given up most of their juice, about 10 minutes. Strain the juice through a fine-mesh sieve into a bowl (to keep the syrup clear instead of cloudy, and therefore better for cocktails, do not press the solids), yielding about 1½ cups. Discard the solids.

2 Return the strawberry juice to the saucepan over medium-low heat, add the sugar, and cook until the sugar dissolves. Add the rose petals and gently simmer 10 minutes. Remove from the heat and strain through a fine-mesh sieve into a bowl, pressing on the petals to extract as much liquid as possible. Stir in the rosewater and set aside to cool. Transfer to an airtight jar and refrigerate.

Make the spritzer:

In a chilled wineglass, combine the wine and strawberry-rose syrup. Top with the seltzer water. Taste and add more syrup if desired. Garnish and serve.

・・・

BANDON BREEZE

Makes 1 serving

This utterly refreshing cocktail pays tribute to the coastal town of Bandon, which is known as the Cranberry Capital of Oregon. The tart red berries have been cultivated there since the late 1800s. This drink is best when made with real fresh cranberry juice. If you can't find fresh cranberry juice, substitute cranberry juice cocktail. If serving a crowd, batch up the mixture and refrigerate. Then set out the pitcher, a bucket of ice, and chilled DRY Sodas, and let everyone mix their own.

Continued

FOR THE CUCUMBER SIMPLE SYRUP

1 cup granulated sugar

1 peeled and grated cucumber

FOR THE COCKTAIL

Ice cubes

2 ounces cucumber simple syrup

1½ ounces vodka

1 ounce high-quality cranberry juice

½ ounce freshly squeezed lime juice

4 ounces cucumber flavor DRY Sparkling Soda

Garnish: cucumber slices or lime wedges

Make the cucumber simple syrup:

In a medium saucepan over medium-high heat, bring 1 cup water and sugar to a simmer. When the sugar has dissolved, remove from the heat and stir in the cucumber. Set aside to cool to room temperature. Strain through a fine-mesh sieve set over a bowl and discard the solids.

Make the cocktail:

Fill a Collins glass three-quarters full with ice. Add the simple syrup, vodka, cranberry juice, and lime juice and stir to combine. Taste and add more syrup if desired. Top with the DRY soda, garnish, and serve.

NORTHWEST SHANDY

Makes 1 serving

Decades ago, Oregon-grown Cascade hops were the secret
behind the uniquely bold and grapefruity India pale ales
of the region's burgeoning craft beer movement. And even
today this hops-forward style defines what we think of as
a Northwest-style IPA. That's why I turn to fresh grapefruit
juice, instead of lemonade, when making a summer shandy.
There's no better match, and even those who think they can't
handle the bitterness of an IPA will love this juicy quencher.

**¾ cup citrusy Northwest-style
IPA beer (I love Fuzzy Tufts Juicy
IPA from Gigantic Brewing)**

**¼ cup freshly squeezed
grapefruit juice**

½ lime

Combine the beer and grapefruit juice in a chilled pint glass. Add a
squeeze of lime and serve.

FULLY LOADED BLOODY MARYS

Makes 1 serving

Loaded with garnishes, this is a Bloody Mary, Portland style.

2 lime wedges

Bloody Mary rim salt (see Note)

Ice cubes

8 ounces tomato juice

2 ounces vodka

1 to 1½ teaspoons extra-hot creamy horseradish

1 teaspoon Worcestershire sauce

½ teaspoon Secret Aardvark hot sauce or Tabasco sauce

¼ teaspoon celery salt

Freshly ground black pepper

Garnish: celery stalk, peeled; 1 skewer with pearl cocktail onions, pepperoncini, olives, cooked shrimp, and hard-cooked quail eggs

1 Slice a slit in 1 of the lime wedges and run it around the rim of a pint glass. Turn the glass upside down and dip it into the rim salt. Fill halfway with ice.

2 In a cocktail shaker, combine the tomato juice, vodka, horseradish, Worcestershire sauce, hot sauce, celery salt, and a few grinds of the black pepper. Add a handful of ice and shake until the outside of the shaker gets frosty, 10 to 20 seconds. Strain over the prepared pint glass. Squeeze the remaining lime wedge over and drop it in. Add another grind of the black pepper and any or all of the garnishes.

Note: If you don't have Bloody Mary rim salt on hand, make your own. In a mortar and pestle, combine 2 tablespoons kosher salt, 1½ teaspoons celery seeds, 1 teaspoon granulated garlic, and 1 teaspoon lemon pepper. Briefly grind until well mixed and a little finer in texture.

FLAMING SPANISH MOCHA

Makes 1 serving

Huber's, Portland's oldest restaurant, has a long and storied history dating back to the late 1800s. But its fiery Spanish Coffee, dramatically concocted tableside, is literally the flame that keeps this old-school slice of history alive. Everyone in town knows there's no better way to warm up on a rainy night than with a hot mug of this boozy brew. My version stays true to the original but adds a spoonful of silky ganache for dessert-like decadence.

¾ ounce overproof or 151 rum

½ ounce triple sec

2 ounces Kahlúa liqueur

3 ounces hot fresh-brewed coffee

1 tablespoon chocolate-coconut ganache (see Note)

Garnish: lightly whipped cream and freshly ground nutmeg

Add the rum and triple sec to a mug or tempered Irish coffee glass and carefully ignite using a lighter or matches. Add the Kahlúa and top with hot coffee, which will extinguish the flames. Stir in the ganache and garnish and serve.

Note: To make the ganache, pour ½ cup hot canned coconut milk or heavy cream over ½ cup chopped dark chocolate or dark chocolate chips in a bowl and stir until melted. Set aside to cool and then refrigerate until firm. Ganache will keep in the refrigerator for several weeks. Try spreading it on toast for a decadent treat.

BROWN BUTTER CHANTERELLE CROSTINI

Makes about 20 crostini

Golden yellow chanterelles grow in abundance in the forests surrounding Portland, and those in the know have their own secret foraging spots. But even if you aren't a forager, you can easily find these delicacies in local markets every spring and fall. I add these buttery beauties to all manner of dishes, but I especially love them simply sautéed with brown butter to let their subtle flavor shine through. Here I've added a touch of cream to increase their luxe quotient.

¾ baguette, cut into ½-inch-thick slices

Olive oil

4 tablespoons (½ stick) unsalted butter

1 large shallot, minced

2 cloves garlic, one cut in half, one minced, divided

1 pound chanterelles, cleaned and roughly chopped

2 teaspoons chopped fresh thyme leaves or more as needed

Kosher salt

Freshly ground black pepper

¼ cup dry vermouth or white wine or more as needed

½ cup heavy cream, plus more to taste

Garnish: freshly grated Parmesan

1 Heat the oven to 425°F. Place a bowl or measuring cup near the stove.

2 Arrange the bread slices on a baking sheet, brush with olive oil, and toast until just golden, about 10 minutes. Rub the cut garlic on each slice twice.

3 In a large sauté pan over medium heat, melt the butter. Cook, stirring occasionally, until the butter smells nutty and the milk solids turn brown. Remove from the heat and strain into the bowl; using a spatula, scrape the brown butter bits out of the pan and into the strainer. Reserve the contents of the strainer.

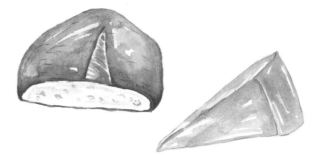

4 Wipe the pan with a paper towel and place over medium-high heat. Add the melted butter and the shallot. Sauté until tender. Add the garlic and sauté 1 minute more. Add the mushrooms and thyme, season with the salt and black pepper, and sauté until the mushrooms are tender and have given off their liquid.

5 Add the vermouth and stir, scraping any brown stuff off the bottom of the pan (add more vermouth if necessary to deglaze the whole pan). Cook until the pan is mostly dry.

6 Stir in the cream and browned butter bits from the strainer and simmer until the mixture is thickened and sauce-like. It if seems dry, add a little more cream. Taste and season with more salt, black pepper, and thyme.

7 Spoon the mixture onto the toasted bread and garnish with the Parmesan.

OYSTERS

with Cucumber Mignonette

Makes 2 to 4 servings

Oysters go by many different names according to the bays or inlets where they grow, but most cultivated in Oregon are of the Pacific variety. Their flavor nuances change depending on the "merrior" of their surrounding waters, but mostly they're characterized by a fresh, cucumber-esque flavor that differentiates them from brinier East Coast oysters. To enhance those crisp vegetal notes, microplaned cucumber is added to a classic mignonette just before serving.

¼ cup red wine vinegar

1 small shallot, finely minced (about 1 tablespoon)

¼ teaspoon freshly ground black pepper

Small pinch of sea or kosher salt

¼ cucumber, peeled, seeded, and finely grated (about 2 tablespoons)

1 dozen freshly shucked oysters

Crushed ice

1 In a small bowl, combine the vinegar, shallot, black pepper, and salt. Set aside at least 10 minutes to allow the shallot to marinate.

2 Arrange the shucked oysters on a plate of crushed ice. Add the grated cucumber to the mignonette, spoon onto the oysters, and serve.

OREGON TRUFFLE GOUGÈRES

Makes 1 dozen

Oregon's native Douglas fir trees provide hospitable ground for white and black truffles. When peak season hits in January, farmers' markets and restaurants are flush with these humble-looking yet highly prized fungi. Like their European counterparts (though far cheaper), Oregon truffles have a musky aroma that exudes decadence. But before you shave a truffle onto your dinner, tuck it in a glass jar with some eggs and butter. Close the lid and refrigerate for a few days while the truffle infuses them with its aroma.

4 tablespoons (½ stick) unsalted butter, preferably truffle infused

½ teaspoon kosher salt

¼ teaspoon freshly ground black pepper

½ cup (spooned and leveled) all-purpose flour

2 large whole eggs (preferably truffle-infused)

3 ounces truffle cheese, such as Gouda, grated (about 1 cup)

¼ ounce shaved fresh truffle (optional)

1 ounce Parmesan, finely grated (about ¼ cup), for sprinkling

1 Heat the oven to 425°F. Line 2 baking sheets with parchment paper.

2 In a large saucepan over medium heat, combine ½ cup water, butter, salt, and black pepper and cook until the butter melts. Add the flour, stirring briskly with a wooden spoon, and cook until the

Continued

mixture pulls away from the sides of the pot and forms a smooth ball. Continue cooking and stirring 1 minute more. Remove from the heat.

3 Transfer to the bowl of a stand mixer fitted with the paddle attachment and beat on medium-low speed until the mixture has cooled down a bit, about 2 minutes. Add the eggs one at a time, beating well after each addition. Mix in the truffle cheese and shaved truffle, if using.

4 Transfer the batter to a large zip-top bag, squeeze out the air, and seal the top. Snip off a corner of the bag and pipe into mounds about the size of large golf balls onto the prepared baking sheets, spacing them about 1 inch apart. Top each mound with a pinch of the Parmesan.

5 Bake 5 minutes and then reduce the heat to 375°F. Bake until golden brown, about 20 minutes more. Remove from the oven.

6 Serve warm.

THE LITTLE LOCAL PORTLAND COOKBOOK

SALADS
AND
SANDWICHES

BUTTER LETTUCE SALAD

with Summer Fruits and Hazelnut Vinaigrette

Makes 4 to 6 servings

Portland summers are perfection. The weather is glorious and the farmers' markets brim with local fruit, lettuces, and Willamette Valley hazelnuts. This salad is a summer celebration meal you can put together after a successful trip to the market.

FOR THE HAZELNUT VINAIGRETTE

3 tablespoons sherry vinegar

1 shallot, finely minced

¾ teaspoon kosher salt

¼ teaspoon freshly ground black pepper

⅓ cup hazelnut oil

FOR THE SALAD

1 head butter lettuce, leaves washed, dried, and torn into bite-sized pieces

2 packed cups baby arugula

Kosher salt

Freshly ground black pepper

4 ounces fresh chèvre (goat cheese), such as Portland Creamery

2 ripe peaches, sliced or diced

¾ cup fresh blueberries

½ cup chopped roasted hazelnuts

Make the hazelnut vinaigrette:

Combine the vinegar, shallot, ¾ teaspoon salt, and ¼ teaspoon black pepper in a small bowl and marinate about 10 minutes. Add the hazelnut oil and whisk until blended. Set aside.

Make the salad:

1 In a bowl, combine the lettuce and arugula. Drizzle with 2 table-spoons vinaigrette and toss, adding more until the leaves are lightly coated and glistening, but not dripping. Taste and season with the salt and black pepper.

2 Crumble the chèvre on top, followed by the peaches, blueberries, and hazelnuts. Drizzle with a little more vinaigrette and serve.

KALE CAESAR SALAD

with Roasted Delicata and Levain Croutons

Makes 4 to 6 servings

You can find infinite varieties of kale salad at restaurants all over Portland. This version pulls influences from two local icons—Nostrana's radicchio salad and Ava Gene's lemony kale Caesar. With tangy levain croutons and roasted delicata squash, it's a hearty salad that's ideal for fall.

FOR THE CAESAR DRESSING

4 anchovy fillets

3 cloves garlic

3 tablespoons mayonnaise

Freshly grated zest and freshly squeezed juice of 1 lemon (about ¼ cup juice)

¾ cup extra virgin olive oil

Kosher salt

FOR THE GARLICKY CROUTONS

6 ounces levain bread, cut into ¾-inch cubes (3 packed cups)

¼ cup extra virgin olive oil

2 cloves garlic, minced

1 teaspoon chopped fresh rosemary

Kosher salt

Freshly ground black pepper

FOR THE SALAD

1 delicata squash, seeded and thinly sliced into half-moons

1 tablespoon extra virgin olive oil

Kosher salt

Freshly ground black pepper

⅛ teaspoon crushed red pepper flakes

1 bunch lacinato kale, stems removed, thinly sliced into shreds, washed and thoroughly dried

⅔ cup lightly packed finely grated Pecorino Romano or Parmesan or a combination

Make the Caesar dressing:

In a food processor, combine the anchovies, garlic, mayonnaise, lemon zest, and lemon juice and process until combined. While the processor is running, pour in ¾ cup olive oil in a steady stream and process until emulsified. Season to taste with the salt.

Make the garlicky croutons:

1 Heat the oven to 425°F.

2 Spread the bread cubes on a baking sheet and bake until toasted, about 10 minutes. (Keep the oven on for the squash.)

3 In a large sauté pan over medium-high heat, warm ¼ cup olive oil. Add the garlic and rosemary and sauté until fragrant, about 1 minute. Remove from the heat and add the toasted bread, tossing until well coated. Season to taste with the salt and black pepper.

Make the salad:

1 Pile the squash on a baking sheet, drizzle with 1 tablespoon olive oil, and season with the salt, black pepper, and red pepper flakes. Toss until well coated. Spread in an even layer and roast until tender and lightly browned on the bottom, about 12 minutes. Turn the squash over and cook until browned on the second side, about 5 minutes more. Remove from the oven.

2 In a large bowl, toss the kale with enough dressing to coat. Taste and season with the salt and black pepper. Set aside about 10 minutes to soften (or massage with your hands for 1 to 2 minutes). Add the roasted delicata, croutons, and most of the cheese (save some for garnish). Drizzle with a bit more dressing and toss to coat. Divide among plates and serve garnished with the remaining cheese.

SALADE NIÇOISE SKEWERS

with Fresh Oregon Albacore

Makes eight 12-inch skewers

Local albacore tuna season is cause for celebration. Seafood cases brim with the pearly pink tuna loins, and restaurants all over town include this firm-fleshed fish on their menus. These gorgeous "salads on a stick" are the perfect way to show it off. They travel well, making them ideal for parties and picnics.

FOR THE LEMON-ANCHOVY VINAIGRETTE

Freshly grated zest and juice of 2 large lemons (about ⅔ cup juice)

½ cup fresh basil leaves

4 anchovies

3 cloves garlic

½ teaspoon freshly ground black pepper

Pinch of kosher salt

⅔ cup extra virgin olive oil

FOR THE SALAD

1 pound fresh Pacific albacore tuna (if loins, cut into 1-inch-thick steaks)

1 pound baby red or gold potatoes (about 8)

¼ cup white wine or chicken or vegetable broth

2 dozen quail eggs

1 tablespoon extra virgin olive oil

1 cup fresh basil leaves, torn if large

1 pint grape tomatoes

1 cup pitted Niçoise olives

Make the vinaigrette:

In the bowl of a food processor or blender, puree the lemon zest and juice, basil, anchovies, garlic, salt, and ½ teaspoon black pepper. With the machine running, drizzle in ⅔ cup olive oil until blended.

Make the salad:

1 Place the tuna in a shallow baking dish, pour the vinaigrette over it, and marinate at room temperature no longer than 30 minutes, turning occasionally. (If you marinate longer, it may cook in the acid of the lemon juice.)

2 Place the potatoes in a pot with well-salted water to cover by 1 inch over medium-high heat and bring to a boil. Cook until tender when pierced with a sharp knife, 8 to 10 minutes. Remove with a slotted spoon and set aside, reserving the water (for a later step).

3 When cool enough to handle, halve the potatoes and transfer to a bowl. Sprinkle with the white wine, or chicken or vegetable broth.

4 Bring the pot of potato water back to a boil over medium-high heat. Add the quail eggs and boil 3 minutes. Remove the eggs with a slotted spoon and transfer to a bowl of cold water. Peel off the shells.

5 Warm a sauté pan over medium-high heat. When hot, add 1 tablespoon olive oil and the marinated fish (do not discard the marinade) and sear until golden brown (but still pink in the center). Transfer to a plate.

6 Pour the marinade into the hot pan and stir to scrape up browned bits, 1 to 2 minutes. Pour into a bowl and set aside.

To assemble the dish:

1 Cut the seared tuna into 1½-inch chunks. Thread eight 12-inch skewers: basil leaf, grape tomato, tuna chunk, olive, potato half, basil leaf, tomato, tuna, olive, quail egg, basil leaf, grape tomato, tuna chunk, olive, potato half, basil leaf, and quail egg. Arrange skewers on a platter and brush or drizzle with the simmered vinaigrette before serving.

EASY HAM AND PÂTÉ BÁNH MÌ

Makes 4 servings

Portland's thriving Vietnamese population has made dishes like pho, bún bò hue, and bánh mì integral parts of the city's food scene, and the many Vietnamese bakeries and markets in town make it easy to prepare these dishes at home. I often make Vietnamese-inspired meatballs to tuck into bánh mì, but when I'm pressed for time I just grab rolls from the Asian market (and a tub of pickled carrots and daikon if I'm really feeling lazy) and fill them with Olympia Provisions Pork Liver Pâté and Sweetheart Ham. The result? Sandwiches that are as fast as they are flavorful.

FOR THE PICKLED CARROTS AND DAIKON (DO CHUA)

1 medium carrot, peeled and cut into matchsticks

1 small daikon, peeled and cut into matchsticks

1 teaspoon kosher salt

1 cup distilled white vinegar

⅓ cup granulated sugar

FOR THE SANDWICHES

4 Vietnamese French bread rolls

½ cup pâté

¼ cup mayonnaise

¼ pound thinly sliced ham

2 jalapeño peppers, sliced

½ cup fresh cilantro leaves

Make the pickled carrots and daikon:

Combine the carrot and daikon in a colander and sprinkle with the salt. Massage the vegetables until they begin to soften and are no longer brittle, about 1 minute. Rinse and place in a 1-quart canning jar. Add the vinegar, 1 cup water, and sugar. Close the lid and shake until the sugar is dissolved. Marinate for at least 1 hour before serving, although longer is better; stores well in the refrigerator for several weeks.

Make the sandwiches:

1 Split each bread roll in half lengthwise so they open like a book. Spread the bottom half of each roll with 2 tablespoons pâté and the top half with a tablespoon of mayonnaise. Layer 2 to 3 ham slices on top of the pâté and add 1 scoop pickled vegetables (being sure to let any excess brine drip off before adding). Top with jalapeño slices and cilantro leaves.

2 Close the sandwiches, slice in half, and serve.

PUB BURGERS

with Bacon and Beer Cheese

Makes 4 burgers

Of all the many brew pubs in Portland, I can't think of a single one that doesn't have a burger on the menu. Burgers and beer just go well together, so why not put a little beer right on the burger itself? A light lager or pilsner adds just the right flavor, without too much hoppy bitterness. Flavorful grass-fed beef from Oregon's local ranches make the best burgers, especially when mixed with a little bacon fat to keep them juicy.

FOR THE BEER CHEESE

4 ounces extra-sharp Cheddar, cut into chunks

1 scallion, ends trimmed, roughly chopped

1 clove garlic

¼ cup lager or pilsner beer, such as pFriem Export Lager

2 tablespoons cream cheese or butter

1 tablespoon Worcestershire sauce

Kosher salt

Freshly ground black pepper

FOR THE BURGERS

4 slices bacon

1⅓ pounds ground grass-fed beef

2 cloves garlic, grated on a fine grater

1 teaspoon kosher salt

1 teaspoon freshly ground black pepper

4 potato buns or other burger buns

Condiments: mustard, mayonnaise, and ketchup

Garnish: lettuce, sliced pickles, sliced tomato, and sliced red or sweet onion

Make the beer cheese:

In the bowl of a food processor, pulse together the cheese, scallion, and garlic until finely chopped. Add the beer, cream cheese, and Worcestershire sauce and process until pureed. Taste and season with the salt and black pepper. Refrigerate until ready to use; beer cheese can be made several days ahead.

Make the burgers:

1 In a sauté pan over medium heat, cook the bacon, turning occasionally, until brown and crisp, about 7 minutes. Remove from the heat. Transfer to a paper towel–lined plate and transfer the bacon grease to a small bowl or measuring cup.

2 In a medium mixing bowl, combine the beef, 1 to 2 tablespoons bacon grease (use the larger amount if the beef is lean), garlic, 1 teaspoon salt, and 1 teaspoon black pepper and mix with your hands until well combined. Shape into 4 burgers about ½ inch thick. Using the back of a spoon, make a shallow 1-inch-wide indentation in the center of each burger. (This will help them cook evenly and prevents them from shrinking.)

3 Heat the grill to medium (350°F to 450° F). Place the burgers on the grill and, with the lid closed, grill until charred on one side and they release easily from the grate, 4 minutes. Turn and cook the other side until a thermometer inserted in the side and pushed all the way to the center reads 155°F, about 4 minutes more. Place the buns, cut sides down, and grill until lightly toasted, about 1 minute.

4 Spread the buns with your choice of the condiments. Place the burgers on the buns, spread each patty with the beer cheese, top with the bacon, and garnish as desired.

MAIN DISHES

BEEF AND ROASTED ROOT STEW

with Black Butte Porter

Makes 6 to 8 servings

The venerable Deschutes Brewing Company, a pioneer of the craft beer movement, created its iconic and beloved Black Butte Porter way back in the 1980s. Its nutty, toasty sweetness adds depth to this rich and beefy stew, but since it's beer, it also adds a few bitter notes. The bright sweetness of the tomato paste and balsamic vinegar brings it all into harmony. Roasting the vegetables separately and adding them toward the end allows them to develop their own deeply caramelized flavor notes.

FOR THE STEW

3 pounds beef chuck, cut into 2-inch chunks

Kosher salt

Freshly ground black pepper

1 tablespoon vegetable oil, plus more as needed

2 large carrots, peeled and diced

1 large onion, diced

4 large cloves garlic, minced

¼ cup tomato paste

5 cups beef stock or broth

1 12-ounce bottle Deschutes Black Butte Porter

1 tablespoon balsamic vinegar

2 bay leaves

1 bouquet garni (6 sprigs fresh thyme, 2 sprigs fresh rosemary, and 1 handful fresh flat-leaf parsley stems tied together with kitchen twine)

5 medium carrots, peeled and
cut into 2-inch chunks

2 Yukon gold potatoes, cut
into 1-inch chunks

1 large turnip, peeled and
cut into 1-inch chunks

1 large rutabaga, peeled and
cut into 1-inch chunks

2 tablespoons extra virgin olive oil

Kosher salt

Freshly ground black pepper

TO FINISH

¼ cup all-purpose flour

3 tablespoons soy sauce or
Bragg Liquid Aminos

Garnish: chopped fresh
parsley or thyme

Make the stew:

1 Season the meat with the salt and black pepper.

2 In a large Dutch oven over medium-high heat, warm the vegetable oil. Working in batches to avoid crowding the pot, brown the meat on all sides, searing until well browned and the meat loosens easily from the pot, 1 to 2 minutes per side. Add more oil if necessary. Transfer the browned meat to a plate.

3 Add the carrot and onion to the Dutch oven and sauté, stirring frequently and scraping up browned bits, until the onions are translucent, about 5 minutes. Add the garlic and sauté 1 minute more.

4 Add the tomato paste, stirring to coat the vegetables, and cook until the tomato paste darkens, about 2 minutes. Add the broth and stir, scraping up the browned bits. Stir in the beer, balsamic vinegar, bay leaves, and bouquet garni and return the meat to the pot. Cover and bring to a simmer.

5 Reduce the heat to low and cook 2 hours. Uncover and continue cooking until the meat is very tender and the liquid is a bit more concentrated, about 1 hour more.

Continued

Make the roasted root vegetables:

1 Heat the oven to 425°F.

2 In a large bowl, toss the carrots, potatoes, turnip, and rutabaga with 2 tablespoons olive oil until coated. Season with the salt and black pepper and toss again.

3 Arrange the vegetables in an even layer on a rimmed baking sheet. Roast until tender and browned, 25 to 30 minutes. Add the roasted vegetables to the stew.

To finish:

1 Combine the flour and soy sauce or Bragg Liquid Aminos in a medium bowl, making a paste. Whisk in 1 to 2 cups of the hot stew liquid and then transfer this mixture to the pot. Simmer until slightly thickened, 5 to 10 minutes. Remove from the heat.

2 Ladle the stew into bowls, garnish as desired, and serve.

DUNGENESS CRAB CIOPPINO

Makes 6 servings

When it's too chilly to sit on the docks at the coast and crack crabs, I get my fix with this show-stopping stew. It gets a spicy hit from diced chunks of Spanish chorizo, which is not to be confused with soft, fresh Mexican chorizo. If you can't find it, use hot link sausage instead. If you boil your own crabs reserve some of the yellow crab "butter" to stir into the soup base for even richer flavor. Serve with crusty bread and salad.

2 teaspoons fennel seeds

2 tablespoons extra virgin olive oil

½ pound Spanish chorizo, diced

1 large onion, diced

3 tablespoons tomato paste

4 cloves garlic, minced

1 cup dry white wine

4 cups fish stock

8 ounces clam juice

1 28-ounce can whole plum tomatoes

¼ cup chopped fresh flat-leaf parsley

2 teaspoons kosher salt

1 teaspoon freshly ground black pepper

1 teaspoon crushed red pepper flakes or to taste

⅛ teaspoon ground allspice

2 bay leaves

1 pound clams, scrubbed (see Note)

1 pound mussels, scrubbed and debearded (see Note)

¼ pound calamari rings and tentacles

1 pound firm white fish, such as halibut or cod, cut into large chunks

½ pound raw large (26/30 count) peeled and deveined shrimp

1 2- to 3-pound cooked and cleaned Dungeness crab, legs removed and cracked, body quartered

Continued

1 Place a large, heavy-bottomed pot over medium-high heat. Add the fennel seeds and toast until fragrant and beginning to color, about 2 minutes. Transfer to a spice grinder or mortar and pestle and grind to a powder.

2 Return the pot to the heat and add the olive oil. Add the chorizo and sauté until the fat renders and it begins to brown, about 5 minutes. Add the onions and sauté until translucent. Push the onions and chorizo to one side, add the tomato paste, and cook about 2 minutes. Stir into the onions. Add the garlic and cook 1 minute more.

3 Deglaze the pot with the wine, scraping up all the browned bits. Add the fish stock and clam juice and then add the plum tomatoes crushing each with your hand as it goes into the pot, along with the juices. Add the parsley, toasted fennel seeds, salt, black pepper, red pepper flakes, allspice, and bay leaves. Cover, raise the heat to high, and bring to a boil.

4 Reduce the heat to medium-low and gently simmer at least 30 minutes.

5 When ready to serve, bring the base to a strong simmer over medium-high heat. Add the clams and mussels, cover, and simmer until the shells have begun to open, about 5 minutes. Add the calamari, fish, and shrimp and simmer until each is opaque throughout, about 5 minutes more. Check for any clams and mussels that aren't completely open and remove and discard them. Add the crab legs and body and heat through, about 2 minutes. Remove from the heat. Remove and discard the bay leaves.

6 Divide cioppino among bowls and serve.

Note: If your clams are wild, soak them in water 30 minutes to 1 hour to encourage them to spit out their sand. To debeard mussels, just grab the "whiskers" and pull until they come out.

NORTHWEST SALMON AND SMOKED TROUT CHOWDER

Makes 6 servings

This chowder is incredibly easy and fast to make, and it's a great way to show off local salmon and smoked trout. Portland-made Thai and True curry paste may seem like an odd addition, but it adds complex flavor in an instant. If you can't find this, substitute your favorite brand of Thai red curry paste. To add a balancing note of acidity, I add a splash of sherry, but white wine works too. Serve with crusty bread and a simple green salad.

2 tablespoons extra virgin olive oil

2 large carrots, peeled and diced

2 large leeks, white and light green parts sliced

½ cup sherry (preferably amontillado) or white wine

6 cups water

3 large Yukon gold potatoes, diced

3 1½-ounce packages concentrated seafood stock, preferably More Than Gourmet (or ¼ cup Better than Bouillon Lobster Base)

2 teaspoons red curry paste, such as Thai and True, plus more as desired

2 teaspoons chopped fresh thyme leaves

Kosher salt

Freshly ground black pepper

1 cup heavy cream

8 ounces smoked trout, skin removed and flaked into bite-sized pieces

12 ounces salmon fillet, skin removed and cut into bite-sized pieces

1 cup fresh or frozen corn kernels (optional)

Continued

1 Warm a large pot or Dutch oven over medium-high heat. When hot, add the oil, carrots, and leeks and sauté, stirring occasionally, until leeks are soft, about 10 minutes.

2 Add the sherry, stirring to scrape up any browned bits on the bottom of the pot. Add the water, potatoes, and seafood concentrate, taking care to get every bit of the concentrate. Stir in the red curry paste and thyme and then season generously with the salt and black pepper. Cover and simmer until potatoes are just tender, about 10 minutes.

3 Add the cream, trout, salmon, and corn, if using, making sure to submerge the salmon in the broth. Simmer until the salmon is cooked through, about 5 minutes. Remove from the heat, taste, and add more salt, pepper, and red curry paste as desired. Serve hot.

CABBAGE, KIELBASA, AND SAUERKRAUT SOUP

Makes 4 servings

Portland is home to one of the biggest populations of Slavic immigrants in the nation, and this soup is inspired by the delicious foodways they've brought to the city. It also serves as a showcase for local hero Olympia Provisions' fantastic kielbasa, which is so good it'll ruin you for any other brand. A healthy spoonful of raw sauerkraut adds beneficial probiotics and gives a nod to our city's longstanding love affair with fermented foods.

1½ teaspoons caraway seeds

12 ounces Polska kielbasa sausage (preferably Olympia Provisions)

1 large onion, chopped

2 large carrots, peeled and diced

1 stalk celery, diced

2 large cloves garlic, minced

6 cups shredded cabbage

6 cups low-sodium chicken broth

1 large russet potato, peeled and diced

¼ cup chopped fresh dill, plus more for garnish

1½ teaspoons smoked paprika

1 teaspoon kosher salt or to taste

¾ teaspoon freshly ground black pepper

Garnish: 1 cup fresh sauerkraut and ⅓ cup sour cream

1 In a small, dry sauté pan over high heat, place the caraway seeds. Toast, stirring occasionally, until the seeds darken, crackle, and just start to smoke. Transfer to a spice grinder or mortar and pestle and grind to a powder.

Continued

2 Cut the kielbasa in half lengthwise and then crosswise into ¼-inch-thick slices. In a large stockpot or Dutch oven over medium-high heat, saute the kielbasa until browned and the fat has rendered, about 5 minutes (if using lean kielbasa, add a teaspoon or two of oil).

3 Add the onion, carrots, and celery and sauté until the onion is softened, about 5 minutes. Add the garlic and sauté 1 minute more. Add the cabbage and cook, stirring occasionally, until slightly wilted, about 3 minutes.

4 Add the chicken broth, potatoes, dill, paprika, toasted caraway powder, fresh dill, salt, and black pepper, raise the heat to high, and bring to a boil.

5 Reduce the heat to medium-low and simmer, uncovered, until the potatoes are tender and the flavors are more concentrated, at least 30 minutes. Remove from the heat.

6 Transfer to serving bowls. Serve each bowl topped with 2 to 4 tablespoons sauerkraut, about 1 tablespoon sour cream, and a sprinkle of dill.

BAKED CHICKEN

with Kale and Cranberry Panade

Makes 4 to 6 servings

This one-pan dinner is inspired by the incredible talents of Portland's many artisan bread bakers, from icons such as Ken Forkish of Ken's Artisan Bakery to the grain geeks at Little T America Baker and Tabor Bread. You can never have too much good bread, but on the rare occasion that you do, repurpose day-old bread into what the French call a panade—basically, a stuffing-like savory bread pudding without the custard. The chicken bakes right on top, bathing everything in its juices.

½ cup dried cranberries

2 tablespoons apple cider vinegar

2 tablespoons extra virgin olive oil, divided, plus more for brushing

1 pound cremini mushrooms, sliced

Kosher salt

Freshly ground black pepper

1 onion, diced

4 large cloves garlic, minced

1½ teaspoons chopped fresh thyme

1 bunch kale, stems removed and coarsely chopped

4 ¾-inch-thick slices day-old artisan bread, cut into cubes (about 1 pound or 6 packed cups)

1 cup chicken broth

6 bone-in, skin-on chicken thighs

1 Heat the oven to 375°F.

2 Combine the cranberries and vinegar in a small microwave-safe bowl and microwave on high 30 seconds or until hot. Stir and set aside.

Continued

3 In a 12-inch cast-iron skillet over medium-high heat, warm 2 teaspoons of the olive oil. Add about half the mushrooms and season with the salt and black pepper. Sauté, stirring occasionally, until the mushrooms begin to give up their liquid. Continue sautéing, turning over occasionally, until seared and golden. Transfer to a bowl or plate and repeat with the remaining mushrooms and 2 more teaspoons of olive oil, removing them to the same bowl once cooked.

4 Warm another 2 teaspoons olive oil in the skillet. Add the onion, season with the salt and black pepper, and sauté until very tender and beginning to caramelize, about 10 minutes. Add the garlic and thyme and sauté 1 minute more. Add the kale and sauté until wilted and tender. Taste and season generously with the salt and black pepper. Add the sautéed mushrooms and bread cubes and stir until evenly combined.

5 In a measuring cup, combine the chicken broth with the cranberries and vinegar and pour the mixture over the ingredients in the skillet. Arrange the chicken thighs on top and season generously with the salt and black pepper.

6 Cover with foil or a lid and bake until the chicken is opaque and almost cooked through, 20 to 30 minutes. Uncover, brush the chicken with olive oil, and bake until the chicken is browned and its internal temperature reaches 165°F, about 15 minutes more.

7 To serve, scoop up a generous serving of panade and a chicken thigh or two onto each plate. Serve.

WILD MUSHROOM AND PANCETTA RISOTTO

Makes 4 to 6 servings

Bolete (aka porcini), chanterelle, and maitake (which is sometimes called Hen of the Woods) are just a few of the mushroom varieties you'll find in the forests and farmers' markets that surround Portland, and they're excellent in this rich risotto. It's baked instead of stirred, so you won't be tied to the stove. Just save a little stock to stir in at the end to loosen the texture.

8 cups chicken stock or low-sodium broth, divided

1 ounce dried or 2 cups diced fresh porcini mushrooms (see Note)

8 ounces diced pancetta

1 pound mixed fresh wild mushrooms, cleaned and chopped

Kosher salt

Freshly ground black pepper

1 large yellow onion, diced

4 large cloves garlic, minced

2 cups carnaroli or arborio rice

¾ cup dry sherry or white wine

4 fresh thyme sprigs

1 bay leaf

½ cup finely grated Parmesan, plus more for serving

2 tablespoons unsalted butter

Garnish: ¼ cup chopped fresh flat-leaf parsley

1 In a saucepan bring the broth to a boil. Remove from the heat and stir in the dried porcini mushrooms, if using. Rehydrate until soft, about 30 minutes. Strain through a fine-mesh sieve set over a large bowl. Rinse the sieve and line with a wet paper towel. Carefully pour the broth through the sieve back into the saucepan. Cover and set over low heat to keep warm.

Continued

2 Rinse the mushrooms to remove any remaining grit. Squeeze them dry and then chop them into small pieces. Set aside.

3 Heat the oven to 350°F.

4 Set a 6-quart Dutch oven over medium-high heat. Add the pancetta and cook until crispy and the fat has rendered, 7 to 10 minutes. Using a slotted spoon, transfer to a paper towel–lined plate. Pour the fat into a small glass measuring cup and set aside.

5 Return the Dutch oven to medium-high heat. Add 1 teaspoon pancetta fat and half the fresh mushrooms, season with salt and black pepper, and sauté until tender, about 5 minutes. Transfer to the plate and repeat with the remaining mushrooms.

6 Return the pot to medium-high heat and add 1 teaspoon pancetta fat and the onion. Season with the salt and black pepper and sauté until tender, about 7 minutes. Add the garlic and sauté 1 minute more.

7 Add the rice to the pot and sauté until translucent around the edges, about 2 minutes. Add the sherry, stirring to scrape up the bits. Once all the liquid is absorbed, add the rehydrated mushrooms, sautéed mushrooms, pancetta, thyme, and bay leaf.

8 Pour in 6 cups of the hot broth, reserving the rest. Season with 1 teaspoon salt and ½ teaspoon black pepper, cover, bring to a simmer, and then transfer to the oven. Bake until the liquid is absorbed, 25 to 30 minutes. Remove from the oven and discard the bay leaf.

9 Stir in the Parmesan, butter, and remaining broth. Taste and season with the salt and black pepper.

Note: If using fresh porcini mushrooms, dice them, season them with the salt and black pepper, and sauté them in 2 teaspoons pancetta fat until golden, about 7 minutes. Transfer to a plate and add to the risotto before baking.

CEDAR-PLANK SALMON

with Pinot Noir Butter

Makes 4 servings

For countless generations, Pacific Northwest tribes have laced salmon fillets to wood stakes and cooked them over a fire, giving the fish a touch of sweet smoke. This tradition has become the centerpiece of the Willamette Valley wine country's world-renowned International Pinot Noir Conference, but home cooks get a similar result by simply laying the fish on a plank of untreated cedar on the grill. It's especially delicious adorned with a scoop of bright Pinot Noir–infused butter.

FOR THE PINOT NOIR BUTTER

1 cup Pinot Noir wine

1 small shallot, finely chopped (about 1 tablespoon)

1 clove garlic

½ teaspoon kosher or truffle salt, such as Jacobsen Salt Co.

¼ teaspoon freshly ground black pepper

1 fresh thyme sprig

4 tablespoons (½ stick) unsalted butter, softened

FOR THE SALMON

1 skin-on salmon fillet (preferably King/Chinook) about 1½ pounds and 1 inch thick, pin bones removed

Extra virgin olive oil as needed

2 teaspoons chopped fresh thyme leaves

1 teaspoon truffle salt, such as Jacobsen Salt Co.

½ teaspoon chopped fresh rosemary

Freshly ground black pepper

Make the pinot noir butter:

1 Combine the wine, shallot, garlic, salt, and ¼ teaspoon black pepper in a small saucepan over medium heat. Cook until reduced to

Continued

¼ cup in volume, 8 to 10 minutes. Remove from the heat and cool to room temperature.

2 In the bowl of a small food processor, whip together the butter, the thyme, and the wine mixture until blended. Transfer to a small container and refrigerate for at least 1 day to allow the flavors to meld.

Make the salmon:

1 Submerge an untreated cedar plank about 15 inches long and 5½ inches wide in water or wine for at least 1 hour.

2 Remove the salmon and Pinot Noir butter from the refrigerator 30 minutes before grilling. Pat the salmon dry with paper towels and brush with the olive oil. Evenly season with the chopped thyme, truffle salt, rosemary, and black pepper.

3 If your grill has a smoker box, place a handful of dry alder or cedar wood chips in it. Prepare the grill for direct cooking over medium heat (350°F to 450°F).

4 Drain the cedar plank, place it over direct heat, and close the lid. After the plank begins to smoke, crackle, and look toasted, about 5 minutes, use long-handled tongs to turn it over. By now, the wood chips should be just starting to smoke. Brush the toasted surface of the plank with the olive oil and slide the salmon, skin side down, onto it. Grill with the lid closed until the salmon is medium rare (125° to 130°F), about 12 minutes. It should be opaque almost all the way through and flake easily.

5 Use grilling mitts to carefully transfer the fillet and plank to a heatproof surface. Use a spatula to cut the fillet into portions and then slide the spatula between the skin and flesh to remove it from the plank. Transfer to a plate and top with a spoonful of the Pinot Noir butter.

BARLEY, KALE, AND FREEKEH BOWLS

with Lemony Tali Sauce

Makes 4 servings

Portland's plethora of creatively minded food carts inspired a nationwide movement, and The Whole Bowl was one of the first on the scene. Serving up just one dish—a healthy brown rice and black bean bowl with an array of toppings—owner Tali Ovadia quickly earned a rabid following thanks to her bright yellow, highly addictive, and savory-tart Tali sauce. This healthy grain bowl recipe pays homage to her creation and to the region's many barley and wheat farmers, too.

FOR THE LEMONY TALI SAUCE

⅓ cup canned or cooked chickpeas

¼ cup extra virgin olive oil

¼ cup nutritional yeast

Freshly grated zest and freshly squeezed juice of 1 lemon (about ¼ cup)

3 cloves garlic

½ teaspoon kosher salt

½ teaspoon dry mustard

¼ teaspoon ground turmeric

⅛ teaspoon cayenne pepper (optional)

FOR THE BOWLS

1 cup pearl barley

Kosher salt

1 cup freekeh or bulgur wheat

2 teaspoons extra virgin olive oil

2 cloves garlic, minced

4 kale leaves, stems removed, chopped

1 tablespoon Bragg Liquid Aminos sauce

Freshly ground black pepper

1 15-ounce can black beans, drained and rinsed

Continued

1 cup shredded Cheddar

½ cup pico de gallo salsa

½ cup sour cream

¼ cup sliced black olives

¼ cup fresh cilantro leaves

1 avocado, sliced

Make the Tali sauce:

Combine all the sauce ingredients in the bowl of a food processor or a blender and puree until smooth. (If sauce seems too thick to pour, thin with a little water.)

Make the bowls:

1 In a saucepan over high heat, combine the barley, 2½ cups water, and a generous pinch of salt and bring to a boil. Reduce the heat to medium-low, cover, and simmer until the barley is tender and the liquid is absorbed, 40 to 50 minutes.

2 In a separate saucepan over high heat, combine the freekeh or bulgur, 2 cups water, and a generous pinch of salt and bring to a boil. Reduce the heat to medium-low, cover, and simmer until tender and the liquid is absorbed, 15 minutes for bulgur and 30 minutes for freekeh. Remove from the heat.

3 In a large sauté pan over medium heat, warm the olive oil. Add the 2 cloves garlic and sauté until fragrant, about 1 minute. Add the kale and Bragg Liquid Aminos sauce, season with the salt and black pepper, and cook until wilted and tender, about 5 minutes. Remove from the heat.

4 Gently mix together the cooked grains and divide them among 4 bowls. Evenly divide the black beans and sautéed kale on top of each bowl. Spoon 2 tablespoons of the lemony Tali sauce on top of each and add the toppings as desired. Serve.

BREAKFAST
AND
BRUNCH

BUCKWHEAT PORRIDGE
with Chai Pear Compote

Makes 6 to 8 servings

Local icon Bob's Red Mill is my source for whole oats and buckwheat. I love to top this soft, nubby porridge with a simple compote of seasonal fruits. In fall, I reach for Oregon's spectacularly sweet and juicy Comice pears simmered in apple cider and spicy chai concentrate from one of Portland's many chai tea makers. A handful of tart dried fruits add more texture and flavor.

FOR THE PORRIDGE

1 cup oat groats

1 cinnamon stick

4 green cardamom pods, crushed

½ teaspoon kosher salt

1 cup buckwheat groats

FOR THE COMPOTE

3 ripe pears, peeled, cored and cut into chunks

½ cup chai tea concentrate

½ cup apple cider

¼ cup packed dark brown sugar, or to taste

½ vanilla bean

1 cup dried cherries, cranberries, or blueberries (preferably a combination)

2 teaspoons lemon juice, or to taste

Kosher salt

FOR THE TOPPINGS

Crème fraîche or Greek yogurt and/or milk as needed

Chopped toasted hazelnuts or other nuts as desired

Make the porridge:

1 In a large saucepan over medium-high heat, combine 8 cups water, oat groats, cinnamon stick, cardamom, and ½ teaspoon salt. Cover and bring to a boil.

2 Reduce the heat to medium-low and simmer 20 minutes. Add the buckwheat groats and cook until the grains are tender, 20 to 30 minutes more. Uncover and continue cooking until any remaining liquid is gone. Remove from the heat and remove and discard the cinnamon stick and cardamom pods.

Make the compote:

1 In a large saucepan over medium-high heat, combine the pears, chai concentrate, apple cider, and brown sugar. Split the vanilla bean in half lengthwise, scrape out the seeds, and add them to the pot, along with the pod. Cover and bring to a simmer.

2 Reduce the heat to medium-low and cook until the pears are tender, 5 to 10 minutes. Uncover, add the dried fruit, and simmer until the fruit is plump and tender and the liquid is syrupy, about 5 minutes more. Taste and add more sugar if desired. Add the lemon juice and season with salt to taste. Remove from the heat.

To serve:

Ladle the porridge into bowls and top each bowl with a spoonful of compote and a dollop of crème fraîche or Greek yogurt and/or a drizzle of milk. Sprinkle with the hazelnuts and serve.

Note: The porridge and compote will keep in the refrigerator for 1 week. Reheat in the microwave or in a pot over low heat (add a little water to keep it from scorching).

Continued

CORNMEAL PANCAKES
with Huckleberry Syrup

Makes about 14 servings

Picking huckleberries along the trails around Mt. Hood is an Oregonian rite of passage. The tiny berries pack a big flavor punch, similar to wild blueberries. Simmered with honey and lavender, they transform into a thick syrup with a floral yet piney aroma that perfectly captures those late-summer hikes. It's fantastic with these fluffy and light hotcakes. Don't skimp on the butter; it makes the pancakes irresistibly moist and accentuates the corn flavor. If you can't find huckleberries or if they are out of season, substitute fresh or frozen regular or wild blueberries.

FOR THE HUCKLEBERRY-LAVENDER SYRUP

3 cups huckleberries or blueberries

½ cup raw honey

½ cup dark brown sugar, densely packed

Freshly grated zest and freshly squeezed juice of 1 lemon (about ¼ cup)

1 teaspoon finely ground dried lavender buds

Pinch of ground cinnamon

Pinch of salt

1¼ cups buttermilk

2 large whole eggs

2 teaspoons vanilla extract

1 cup finely ground cornmeal

1 cup all-purpose flour
(spooned and leveled)

¼ cup packed dark brown sugar

1 teaspoon baking powder

½ teaspoon baking soda

¼ teaspoon kosher salt

5 tablespoons unsalted
butter, melted

Vegetable oil as needed

Crispy cooked bacon for serving

Make the huckleberry-lavender syrup:

In a medium saucepan over medium heat, combine all the syrup ingredients plus ¼ cup water and bring to a simmer. Cook, mashing with a spoon, until the berries are soft and the juices have begun to thicken, 10 to 15 minutes. Remove from the heat and strain through a fine-mesh sieve into a large glass measuring cup, pressing on the solids to discharge all of the juices. Discard the solids. If the syrup seems a little thin, return to the saucepan over medium heat and simmer a few minutes more. It will also thicken as it cools. Cover to keep warm until ready to serve.

Make the pancakes:

1 In a medium bowl or large measuring cup, combine the buttermilk, eggs, and vanilla extract until well blended.

2 In a large mixing bowl, combine the cornmeal, flour, ¼ cup brown sugar, baking powder, baking soda, and salt. Stir the liquid ingredients into the dry ingredients until just combined. Stir in the melted butter. Let the batter rest and thicken for up to 10 minutes while you heat the griddle.

Continued

3 Heat the oven to 250°F and place a baking sheet on the center rack to keep the pancakes warm until ready to serve.

4 Warm a griddle or skillet over medium heat, lightly coating it with oil if necessary and wiping off any excess. Working in batches, use a ¼ cup measure to pour the batter for each pancake. Cook each until the bottoms are golden and the edges are beginning to look set, about 1½ minutes. Turn and cook on the second side until golden, about 1 minute more.

5 Transfer the cooked pancakes to the baking sheet in the oven to keep warm. Repeat with the remaining batter until all has been used.

6 Serve hot with the warm huckleberry-lavender syrup and crispy bacon.

SALMON HASH

with Double-Mustard Vinaigrette

Makes 4 servings

When I'm making salmon, I always make extra so I can use the leftovers in dishes like omelets, scrambled eggs, and this hash. It's hearty enough to stand in for dinner, especially with a poached egg on top. The mustardy vinaigrette ties all the flavors together.

FOR THE MUSTARD VINAIGRETTE

1 tablespoon Dijon mustard

2 teaspoons whole grain mustard

1 tablespoon sherry vinegar
or red wine vinegar

1 tablespoon extra virgin olive oil

1 teaspoon prepared horseradish

FOR THE HASH

1½ pounds Yukon gold
potatoes, cut into cubes

4 ounces bacon, diced

2 tablespoons vegetable oil,
plus more as needed

1 medium yellow onion,
chopped (about ¾ cup)

½ diced green bell pepper

Kosher salt

Freshly ground black pepper

2 large cloves garlic, minced

8 ounces cooked or cold-smoked
salmon (not lox), skin and
bones removed and flaked

2 scallions, thinly sliced

2 tablespoons chopped fresh parsley

Make the vinaigrette:

In a small bowl, whisk together the mustards, vinegar, olive oil, and horseradish. Set aside.

Continued

Make the hash:

1 Place the potatoes in a large pot and cover with water by 1 inch. Cover, place over high heat, and bring to a boil.

2 Uncover, reduce the heat to medium-low, and simmer until the potatoes are easily pierced with a fork, about 5 minutes. Remove from the heat, drain, and set aside to cool.

3 In a large skillet over medium-high heat, cook the bacon until crisp, about 5 minutes. Using a slotted spoon, transfer to a paper towel–lined plate to drain, leaving behind as much fat as possible.

4 Return the skillet to medium-high heat (if there is less than 1 tablespoon of fat in the pan, add a little of the vegetable oil). Add the onion and green pepper and season with the salt and black pepper. Sauté, stirring occasionally, until tender, about 5 minutes. Add the garlic and sauté about 1 minute more. Transfer the contents of the skillet to a bowl.

5 Return to medium-high heat and add 1 tablespoon vegetable oil. Add the potatoes and season generously with the salt and black pepper. Cook, undisturbed, until browned on one side, about 5 minutes. Turn and brown the other side, adding the remaining 1 tablespoon vegetable oil, about 5 minutes more.

6 Add the onion mixture, bacon, flaked salmon, and scallions to the skillet and sauté, stirring gently, until salmon is heated through. Add the vinaigrette and stir until evenly coated. Remove from the heat.

7 Divide the hash among 4 plates and garnish with the parsley. Serve.

BAKED APPLE CIDER DOUGHNUTS

*Makes 1 dozen regular-sized doughnuts or
2 dozen mini doughnuts*

Every fall and winter, Oregon's pumpkin patches and Christmas tree farms trot out their mini doughnut fryers to offer visitors warm, made-to-order apple cider doughnuts. When you're cold, muddy, and tired of hauling around a heavy tree, there is truly nothing better than a hot doughnut. These baked doughnuts are just as delicious and don't require vats of oil. To mimic the decadence of fried doughnuts, they're brushed with melted butter and then rolled in spiced sugar.

FOR THE DOUGHNUTS

1 cup fresh apple cider

2 cups all-purpose flour
(spooned and leveled)

2 teaspoons baking powder

2 teaspoons ground cinnamon

1 teaspoon ground ginger

½ teaspoon baking soda

½ teaspoon kosher salt

¼ teaspoon ground allspice

⅛ teaspoon freshly ground nutmeg

2 large whole eggs

¾ cup packed dark brown sugar

½ cup apple butter or sour cream

¼ cup melted coconut
oil or vegetable oil

1½ teaspoons vanilla extract

FOR THE TOPPING

¾ cup granulated sugar

3 teaspoons ground cinnamon

1½ teaspoons ground allspice

8 tablespoons (1 stick)
unsalted butter, melted

Continued

1 Heat the oven to 350°F. Lightly grease two regular or two mini doughnut pans.

2 In a small saucepan over medium-high heat boil the apple cider until reduced to ½ cup, 3 to 5 minutes. Remove from the heat and set aside to cool while you prepare the other ingredients.

3 In a medium mixing bowl, whisk together the flour, baking powder, 2 teaspoons cinnamon, ginger, baking soda, salt, ¼ teaspoon allspice, and nutmeg.

4 In a separate mixing bowl, whisk together the eggs, brown sugar, apple butter, oil, and vanilla extract until smooth. Stir in the cooled apple cider.

5 Stir the wet ingredients into the dry ingredients until just combined.

6 Spoon the batter into a large zip-top bag. Squeeze out the air and seal the top. Snip off a corner of the bag and use it to pipe the batter into the prepared pans, filling each cup ¾ full. (Piping with a bag helps ensure you don't overfill the pans, which would close up the doughnuts' holes.)

7 Bake until the tops spring back when lightly pressed, 10 to 15 minutes for regular-sized doughnuts or 8–10 minutes for mini doughnuts. Remove from the oven and set aside to cool a few minutes before removing from the pans.

Make the topping:

1 In a shallow bowl, stir together the granulated sugar, 2 teaspoons cinnamon, and 1 teaspoon allspice, or process them in the bowl of a food processor if you prefer the texture of superfine sugar.

2 Brush each doughnut with the butter and then toss in the sugar mixture to coat. (Skip the butter step if you're feeling virtuous; the doughnuts are moist enough for the sugar to adhere.)

Note: Though these doughnuts are best eaten the day they're made, they're so moist and tender they'll keep in an airtight container for up to 3 days. Just wait to top them with the butter and sugar until you're ready to serve.

DESSERTS

OREGON SNOWBALL COOKIES

Makes about 4 dozen

The classic Russian tea cake gets an Oregon twist with the addition of chopped fir needles and brandy. One of Portland's first craft distilleries, Clear Creek Distillery, got its start back in 1985 and became famous for its pear-in-the-bottle eau de vie. Its Douglas Fir brandy, which I boil to reduce its alcohol content, adds a delicate, evocative evergreen note to these cookies. It's almost more scent than taste, like a winter hike in cookie form. If you can't get your hands on the brandy, see the Note below.

½ cup Clear Creek Distillery Douglas Fir Brandy or other brandy (see Note)

1½ cups toasted hazelnuts

½ pound (2 sticks) unsalted butter

1½ cups confectioners' sugar, divided

2 tablespoons finely minced fresh fir tree needles (see Note)

1 teaspoon vanilla extract

½ teaspoon kosher salt

2½ cups all-purpose flour (spooned and leveled)

1 Heat the oven to 400°F. Line 2 baking sheets with parchment paper.

2 In a small saucepan over medium-high heat, bring the brandy to a boil.

3 Reduce the heat to medium-low and simmer until reduced by half, to ¼ cup. Remove from the heat and set aside to cool.

4 In a food processor or by hand, finely chop the hazelnuts. Set aside.

5 In a food processor or a stand mixer fitted with the paddle attachment, process or beat the butter, ½ cup confectioners' sugar, and minced fir needles until light and fluffy. Add the cooled brandy, vanilla extract, and salt and pulse or mix to combine. Add the flour and nuts and pulse or mix until fully incorporated.

6 Shape the dough into 1-inch balls and arrange on the baking sheets (place them about 1 inch apart; they don't spread). Bake until just barely beginning to brown, 10 to 12 minutes.

7 Allow cookies to cool slightly and then roll them in the remaining confectioners' sugar. When completely cool, roll again. Serve or store in an airtight container.

Note: I happen to have a true fir tree in my backyard, but if you don't, look around the neighborhood or go for a walk. Just don't use your Christmas tree, unless you know for certain it hasn't been sprayed. If you use Douglas fir needles, keep in mind that they're more potent.

Note: For a brandy-free variation, in a food processor, process ½ cup granulated sugar with 2 tablespoons chopped fir needles until the needles are reduced to fine particles and blended into the sugar. Roll the baked cookies in the sugar while still slightly warm. When completely cool, roll in the confectioners' sugar.

ALMOND-MATCHA MADELEINES

with Cardamom

Makes about 2 dozen madeleines

The hometown of behemoths like Stash and Tazo, not to mention dozens of beloved artisan tea and kombucha makers, Portland has had a long love affair with all things related to tea. These tender little cakes celebrate that heritage with green tea powder, plus ground cardamom for a welcome hint of earthiness. If you don't have almond flour, you can grind whole or sliced almonds in a food processor until very fine. It will be a little coarser than store-bought, but it still works great.

Unsalted butter for greasing the pans

½ cup all-purpose flour (spooned and leveled), plus more for the pans

½ cup almond flour

1 tablespoon matcha powder, such as Mizuba Tea Co.

½ teaspoon kosher salt

3 green cardamom pods (or ⅛ teaspoon ground cardamom)

2 large whole eggs, at room temperature

½ cup granulated sugar

½ teaspoon vanilla extract

12 tablespoons (1½ sticks) unsalted butter, melted and cooled

1 Heat the oven to 400°F. Generously butter and flour two madeleine pans (alternatively, you can use mini muffin pans and bake at 350°F).

2 In a small mixing bowl, combine the flours, matcha powder, and salt.

3 Break open the cardamom pods to extract the seeds and crush the seeds in a mortar and pestle until ground into about ⅛ teaspoon of fine powder (alternatively, you can use ground cardamom, but it won't be quite as fragrant). Add to the flour mixture.

4 In the bowl of a stand mixer fitted with the paddle attachment, beat together the eggs and sugar on high speed until thickened and very light in color (when you lift the beater, the mixture should fall like ribbons back into the bowl), about 4 minutes. Beat in the vanilla extract. With the mixer on low, stir in the flour mixture. Add the melted butter and stir just until combined. Set aside until it begins to thicken up, about 10 minutes (or refrigerate up to overnight to produce madeleines with a signature hump).

5 Spoon a generous tablespoon of batter into each of the prepared madeleine molds. Bake until the edges are browned and the tops spring back when lightly pressed, about 10 minutes. If using mini muffin pans, fill the cups about two-thirds full and bake at the lower temperature for a few minutes longer. Remove from the oven and set aside to cool.

SKILLET MARIONBERRY-BLUEBERRY COBBLER

Makes 8 to 10 servings

Considered the "Cabernet of blackberries," marionberries offer a complex sweet-tart flavor that earns them star status. The hybrid berry, developed at Oregon State University in the 1950s, now accounts for more than half the state's blackberry production. Here, they're paired with sweet blueberries in a biscuit-topped cobbler that's perfect for summer.

FOR THE BISCUITS

3 cups all-purpose flour (spooned and leveled)

1 tablespoon baking powder

1 tablespoon granulated sugar, plus more for sprinkling

1 teaspoon kosher salt

8 tablespoons (1 stick) unsalted butter, very cold and cut into ¼-inch cubes

1¼ cups heavy cream, half-and-half, or milk

Melted butter for brushing

FOR THE FILLING

6 cups fresh marionberries or blackberries

3 cups fresh blueberries

½ cup granulated sugar

3 tablespoons cornstarch

Vanilla ice cream for serving

Make the biscuits:

1 In a large bowl, whisk together the flour, baking powder, 1 tablespoon sugar, and salt. Cut in the butter using a pastry blender or forks until the mixture looks a bit like cornmeal scattered with some larger pieces of butter. (Alternatively, use a food processor.)

2 Make a well in the center of the flour and add the cream. Fold the dry ingredients into the wet ingredients until a shaggy dough forms. Turn out onto a lightly floured surface and briefly knead into a cohesive mass.

3 Pat the dough out into a large rectangle. Fold the sides of the dough over on itself like you're folding a letter, and then fold again in half. Pat it out again and repeat. (This process helps create flaky layers.) Pat the dough into a ¾-inch- to 1-inch-thick circle and cut into rounds using a 2 ½-inch biscuit cutter. Gently push the scraps together and cut out more (you should get about 8 or 9 in all).

4 Arrange the biscuits on a parchment-lined baking sheet, cover with plastic wrap, and freeze for at least 15 minutes while preparing the filling.

Make the filling:

1 Heat the oven to 375°F. In a large bowl, combine the marionberries, blueberries, sugar, and cornstarch. Pour into a large cast-iron skillet or baking dish and bake until bubbling, 20 minutes. Remove from the oven and raise the heat to 425°F.

2 Arrange the frozen biscuits on top of the hot fruit. Brush the tops with the melted butter, sprinkle with the extra sugar, and bake until biscuits are golden brown and cooked through, 20 minutes more.

3 Serve warm with the vanilla ice cream, of course.

Note: You can also freeze the biscuits and then pack them into zip-top bags to bake up whenever a craving strikes. If baking the biscuits on their own, heat oven to 425°F. Arrange the frozen biscuits in a buttered baking dish just big enough to hold them. Brush the tops with melted butter and bake until golden brown, 15 to 20 minutes.

RICH MOCHA PUDDINGS
with Boozy Whipped Cream

Makes 8 servings

Portland's not called Drip City for nothing—and no, it's not just because of the rain. A vanguard of the Third Wave coffee movement, the city is home to more artisan coffee roasters per capita than almost any other, and our bean-to-bar artisan chocolate scene isn't far behind. These rich, silky custards celebrate Portland's delicious dexterity with both kinds of beans.

FOR THE MOCHA PUDDING

⅔ cup dark brown sugar, densely packed

¼ cup freshly brewed espresso

¼ cup cornstarch

3 tablespoons unsweetened cocoa powder

1 teaspoon kosher salt

2¾ cups half-and-half

3½ ounces bittersweet chocolate (70% cacao), finely chopped

1½ teaspoons vanilla extract

FOR THE BOOZY WHIPPED CREAM

1 cup heavy cream, very cold

1 teaspoon vanilla extract

1 tablespoon confectioners' sugar

1 tablespoon bourbon (optional; or omit vanilla extract, confectioners' sugar, and bourbon and use 2 tablespoons Frangelico liqueur)

Make the mocha pudding:

1 In a medium bowl, mix together the brown sugar, espresso, corn-starch, cocoa powder, and salt until well combined.

2 In a medium saucepan over medium heat, bring the half-and-half just to a simmer. Very slowly and while whisking constantly, pour the hot half-and-half into the cornstarch mixture. Transfer the mixture to the saucepan, return to heat, and cook, stirring continuously but not furiously, until the mixture comes to a low boil, is thick, and bubbles begin to pop on the surface.

3 Reduce the heat to medium-low and cook, stirring constantly, 1 minute more. The mixture should be very thick, like pudding. Remove from the heat and add the chocolate and vanilla extract, stirring until smooth.

4 Divide the mixture among 8 ramekins. Place a sheet of plastic wrap directly on the surface of each to prevent a skin from forming. Refrigerate until cold, at least 3 hours.

Make the boozy whipped cream:

1 In the bowl of a stand mixer fitted with the whisk attachment, combine the cream, vanilla extract, confectioners' sugar, and bourbon (or just the cream and Frangelico). Beat until the cream holds medium-soft peaks. (Alternatively, you can whisk by hand.)

2 Serve each of the puddings topped with a dollop of the whipped cream.

ACKNOWLEDGMENTS

Nothing pairs better with good food than good friends, and I'm so thankful to have had the pleasure of eating most of the recipes in this book with my wonderful friend, blog co-conspirator, and photographer extraordinaire, Wendi Nordeck. This book wouldn't exist without you, Wendi, and I'm so grateful for our friendship.

Another big shout out goes to my mentor and friend, Martha Holmberg, who has taught me so much over the years, and graciously opened the door to this project.

Big thanks to Leslie Jonath for believing in me and being such a smart, careful, and sensitive editor. You made this project a joy from start to finish. And to Courtney Jentzen for the fantastic illustrations that infuse the book with so much Portland spirit. Thanks Debbie Berne for the design and the crew at The Countryman Press for making it all happen.

And of course, I'm forever grateful to my husband, Mike, and daughters, Emma and Audrey. They're the most honest, faithful—and patient—taste-testers a cookbook author could ask for.

Courtney Jentzen would like to thank Carly Martin for her help with the illustrations. Thanks also to Redding, Stevie, and Paul.

INDEX

Almond-Matcha
  Madeleines with
  Cardamom, 72–73
Apple Cider Doughnuts,
  Baked, 65–67

Bandon Breeze, 13–14
Bánh Mì, Easy Ham and
  Pâté, 32–33
Barley, Kale, and Freekeh
  Bowls, 53–55
beef
  Beef and Roasted Root
    Stew with Black
    Butte Porter, 38–40
  Pub Burgers with Bacon
    and Beer Cheese,
    34–35
beer
  Beef and Roasted Root
    Stew with Black
    Butte Porter, 38–40
  Northwest Shandy, 15
  Pub Burgers with Bacon
    and Beer Cheese,
    34–35
Bloody Marys, Fully
  Loaded, 16
blueberries
  Butter Lettuce Salad
    with Summer
    Fruits, 26–27
  Skillet Marionberry-
    Blueberry Cobbler,
    74–75
brandy
  Oregon Snowball
    Cookies, 70–71
bread
  Brown Butter
    Chanterelle
    Crostini, 18–19
  Kale and Cranberry
    Panade, 47–48

Buckwheat Porridge with
  Chai Pear Compote,
  58–59
Burgers, Pub, with Bacon
  and Beer Cheese,
  34–35

Cabbage, Kielbasa, and
  Sauerkraut Soup,
  45–46
Caesar Salad, Kale, 28–29
cheese
  Oregon Truffle
    Gougères, 21–22
  Pub Burgers with Bacon
    and Beer Cheese,
    34–35
Chicken, Baked, with
  Kale and Cranberry
  Panade, 47–48
chocolate
  Flaming Spanish
    Mocha, 17
  Rich Mocha Puddings,
    76–77
Chowder, Northwest
  Salmon and Smoked
  Trout, 43–44
Cioppino, Dungeness
  Crab, 41–42
Cobbler, Skillet
  Marionberry-
  Blueberry, 74–75
coffee
  Flaming Spanish
    Mocha, 17
  Rich Mocha Puddings,
    76–77
Cookies, Oregon
  Snowball, 70–71
Crab Cioppino,
  Dungeness, 41–42
Crostini, Brown Butter
  Chanterelle, 18–19

Doughnuts, Baked Apple
  Cider, 65–67
drinks
  Bandon Breeze, 13–14
  Flaming Spanish
    Mocha, 17
  Fully Loaded Bloody
    Marys, 16
  Northwest Shandy, 15
  Rosy Wine Spritzers,
    12–13

fish
  Cedar-Plank Salmon
    with Pinot Noir
    Butter, 51–52
  Dungeness Crab
    Cioppino, 41–42
  Northwest Salmon
    and Smoked Trout
    Chowder, 43–44
  Salade Niçoise Skewers
    with Fresh Oregon
    Albacore, 30–31
  Salmon Hash with
    Double-Mustard
    Vinaigrette, 63–64
Flaming Spanish Mocha, 17
Freekeh Bowls, Barley,
  Kale, and, with
  Lemony Tahi Sauce,
  53–55

Ham and Pâté Bánh Mì,
  Easy, 32–33
Huckleberry-Lavender
  Syrup, 60–61

Kahlúa
  Flaming Spanish
    Mocha, 17
kale
  Barley, Kale, and
    Freekeh Bowls, 53–55

kale (*continued*)
  Kale and Cranberry
    Panade, 47–48
  Kale Caesar Salad,
    28–29

Lettuce Salad, Butter,
  with Summer
  Fruits, 26–27

Madeleines, Almond-
  Matcha, with
  Cardamom, 72–73
Marionberry-Blueberry
  Cobbler, Skillet,
  74–75
mushrooms
  Baked Chicken with
    Kale and Cranberry
    Panade, 47–48
  Brown Butter
    Chanterelle
    Crostini, 18–19
  Wild Mushroom and
    Pancetta Risotto,
    49–50

Northwest Shandy, 15

Oysters with Cucumber
  Mignonette, 20

Pancakes, Cornmeal, with
  Huckleberry Syrup,
  60–62
Pancetta Risotto, Wild
  Mushroom and,
  49–50
peaches
  Butter Lettuce Salad
    with Summer
    Fruits, 26–27
Pear Compote, Chai,
  Buckwheat Porridge
  with, 58–59
Puddings, Rich Mocha,
  76–77

Risotto, Wild Mushroom
  and Pancetta, 49–50
rum
  Flaming Spanish
    Mocha, 17

sausage
  Cabbage, Kielbasa,
    and Sauerkraut
    Soup, 45–46
seafood. *See also* fish
  Dungeness Crab
    Cioppino,
    41–42
squash
  Kale Caesar Salad
    with Roasted
    Delicata,
    28–29

Truffle Gougères, Oregon,
  21–22

vodka
  Bandon Breeze, 13–14
  Fully Loaded Bloody
    Marys, 16

wine
  Pinot Noir Butter, 51
  Rosy Wine Spritzers,
    12–13